the Knitter's Handbook

The Knitter's Handbook PUBLISHED BY XRX BOOKS

credits

PUBLISHER
Alexis Yiorgos Xenakis

COEDITORS
Rick Mondragon
Elaine Rowley

EDITORIAL ASSISTANT
Sue Nelson

TECHNICAL EDITOR
Joni Coniglio

TECHNICAL ASSISTANT
Cole Kelley

GRAPHIC DESIGNER
Bob Natz

PHOTOGRAPHER
Alexis Xenakis

SECOND PHOTOGRAPHER
Mike Winkleman

DIRECTOR, PUBLISHING SERVICES
David Xenakis

TECHNICAL ILLUSTRATOR
Carol Skallerud

FASHION ILLUSTRATOR
Natalie Sorenson

PRODUCTION DIRECTOR &
COLOR SPECIALIST
Dennis Pearson

BOOK PRODUCTION MANAGER
Susan Becker

DIGITAL PREPRESS
Everett Baker
Jay Reeve

MIS
Jason Bittner

FIRST PUBLISHED IN USA IN 2005 BY XRX, INC.

COPYRIGHT © 2005 XRX, INC.

ISBN 1-893762-21-1
Produced in Sioux Falls, South Dakota, by XRX, Inc.,
PO Box 1525, Sioux Falls, SD 57101-1525 USA 605.338.2450

a publication of XRX BOOKS

Visit us online at www.knittinguniverse.com

welcome

Like everyone else, knitters live in the Information Age. And, like everyone else, we are all beneficiaries and victims of a bountiful time.

As the books, magazines, videos, and web digests stack up, it becomes more difficult, not easier, to put our hands on what we need when we need it.

During our knitting time, most of us don't need a wagonload of technique books, we just need one that does the job—one that is compact, concise, and convenient.

Let *The Knitter's Handbook* be your choice.

Since our goal is to give easy access to the essential skills, you'll find a detailed table of contents with a Quick Access listing; sections arranged alphabetically; a ticker tape highlighting the section title on each page; and a complete index to boot.

As you go along through a rich and full knitting life, you'll want to add to your *Handbook*. That's what the note pages at the end of each section are for; there's even one at the back of the book for your own indexed entries.

Grab your knitting and see how easy it is—
    to cast on in pattern (page 38),
    to shape shoulders with refined short rows (page 96),
    to do it all,
    —with the confidence and support you need.

table of contents

Basics

BASICS - abbreviations and terms

[]   Work instructions inside brackets as many times as directed

*   Repeat instructions following the asterisk(s) as directed

"   inch(es)

approx   **approximately**

back The side of the knitting that is away from the knitter

Back The section of a garment that is worn to the back of the body

beg   **begin(ing)(s)**

binding off Removing a stitch from the needle and securing it, usually by passing it over another stitch

blocking Applying moisture to the knit fabric and allowing it to dry flat to set the stitches

casting on Forming the initial stitch

CC   **contrasting color**

cm   **centimeter(s)** Measure of length equaling .4 of inches

cn   **cable needle**

dec   **decreas(e)(ed)(es)(ing)** Removing a stitch by making 2 or more stitches into 1

dpn   **double-pointed needle(s)** Needle with a point at each end

front The side of the knitting facing the knitter

Front The section of a garment worn to the front of the body

foll   **follow(ing)(s)**

g   **gram(s)** Measure of weight equaling .035 ounce

garter stitch The fabric produced by knitting all stitches, all rows

gauge The number of stitches and rows worked in 10 centimeters/4 inches

inc   **increas(e)(ed)(es)(ing)** Adding a stitch by making 1 stitch into 2 or more

k   **knit(ting)(s)(ted)**

k2tog   **knit 2 together** Knit 2 stitches as if they were 1 (a right-slanting decrease)

k tbl   **knit into the back of a stitch** Knit into the part of the stitch on the back of the needle

kf&b   **knit into the front and back of a stitch** Knit into the front and then the back of the same stitch (1 stitch becomes 2 stitches)

k-wise   **knitwise** As if to knit

Left (Back, Front, or Sleeve) The section of a garment worn on the left side of the body

LH   **left-hand needle** The needle held in your left hand.

live stitches Stitches that are ready to be worked: they have not been bound off

m   **meter(s)** Measure of length equaling 1.1 yards

M1   **Make 1** Increase by picking up the thread between the needles and working into the back of it

mc   **main color**

mm   **millimeter(s)** Measure of length equaling .04 inches

oz   **ounce(s)** Measure of weight equaling 28 grams

p   **purl(ed)(ing)(s)**

pat   **pattern(s)** A repeating arrangement of knits and purls and other operations that form a knit fabric

picking up Forming a stitch by inserting needle into a finished edge and placing a loop from the knit fabric on the needle

picking up and knitting Forming a stitch by inserting needle into a finished edge and using yarn to knit a new stitch, usually done to add a border onto a piece

pm   **place marker**

psso   **pass slipped stitch over**

p-wise   **purlwise** As if to purl

Right (Back, Front, or Sleeve) The section of a garment worn on the right side of the body

rem   **remain(ing)(s)**

BASICS - abbreviations and terms

rep   **repeat(s)**

rev St st

reverse stockinette stitch The bumpy fabric that is produced by purling all stitches on right-side rows and knitting all stitches on wrong-side rows

RH   **right hand needle** The needle held in your right hand

ridge The horizontal line in garter-stitch fabric produced by knitting 2 rows

rnd   **round** Working once around a piece of circular knitting

row Working once across a piece of flat knitting

RS   **right side** The 'public' side of a knit fabric

selvage/selvedge The edge stitch or stitches added to a pattern to facilitate seaming

sc   **single crochet**

short row Partial rows worked within a piece, see pages 96 and 97

SKP   **slip 1, knit 1, pass slip stitch over** Slip 1 stitch from left needle knitwise, knit the next stitch, then pass the slipped stitch over the knit stitch (a left-slanting decrease)

sl 1 k-wise

slip 1 knit-wise Slip the next stitch from left needle, as if to knit

sl 1 p-wise

slip 1 purl-wise Slip the next stitch from left needle, as if to purl

ssk   **slip, slip, knit** A left-slanting decrease, see page 61

ssp   **slip, slip, purl** A left-slanting decrease, see page 61

sl st   **slip stitch** A stitch formed by transferring it from left needle to right needle without working it

st(s)   **stitch(es)** Loop(s) formed with yarn on the knitting needles

St st   **stockinette stitch** The smooth fabric that is produced by knitting all stitches on right-side rows and purling all stitches on wrong-side rows

tail The yarn left hanging at the beginning or end of a ball or piece

tbl   **through the back loop** See page 6

tog   **together**

turn Turn work to opposite side

work even Continue on the same number of stitches (no increasing or decreasing)

working flat Working a row, turning the piece, then working the next row

working in rounds Working a row with circular or double-pointed needles, then working the next row without turning the piece (also known as *working circularly*)

working yarn The length of yarn being used to knit, not the 'tail'

wyib   **with yarn in back** With working yarn on the side of the knitting that is away from the knitter

wyif   **with yarn in front** With working yarn on the side of the knitting that faces the knitter

WS   **wrong side(s)** The 'non-public' side(s) of the garment

yarn Synonymous with 'working yarn'; the length of yarn being used to knit, not the 'tail'

yd   **yard** Measure of length equaling 36" (.9144 meter)

yo   **yarn-over** An extra stitch created by bringing yarn over the needle, producing a hole in the knitting

BASICS
KNIT (K)

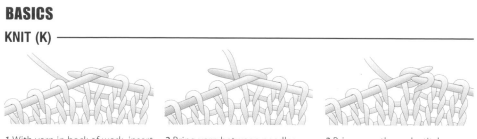

1 With yarn in back of work, insert right needle into stitch on left needle from front to back.

2 Bring yarn between needles and over right needle.

3 Bring yarn through stitch with right needle. Pull stitch off left needle.

4 Knit stitch completed.

Stockinette stitch, knit side: Alternate a knit row and a purl row.

Garter stitch: Knit every row.

KNIT IN REVERSE (OR KNIT BACK BACKWARDS)

Alternate a row of knit (worked from right to left) with a row of knit in reverse (worked from left to right) to produce stockinette stitch fabric without turning the work or purling. This method is perfect for small areas (bobbles, entrelac) and ambidextrous knitters. Some left-handed knitters may choose to always knit in reverse and purl in reverse.

1 With yarn in back of work, insert left needle into stitch on right needle from front to back and move left needle behind right needle.

2 Bring yarn over left needle tip from back to front.

3 While lifting right needle tip, bring yarn through stitch and onto left needle to form new stitch. Pull stitch off right needle.

BASICS

PURL (P)

1 With yarn in front of work, insert right needle into stitch from back to front.

2 Bring yarn over right needle from front to back.

3 Bring yarn through stitch with right needle. Pull stitch off left needle. Repeat Steps 1–3.

STITCH ORIENTATION

If a stitch does sit on the needle the wrong way, work into it as follows:

This way   *Not this way*

It's essential to understand that every stitch should sit on the needle the correct way. The yarn coming from the previous stitch (the loop's right leg) is at the front of the needle. The yarn going to the following stitch (the loop's left leg) is at the back of the needle.

To knit the stitch
Insert right needle into stitch from front to back and knit stitch.

To purl the stitch
Insert needle into stitch from back to front and purl stitch.

PURL IN REVERSE (OR PURL BACK BACKWARDS)

 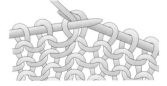 

1 With yarn in front of work, insert left needle into stitch on right needle from back to front.

2 Wrap yarn counterclockwise around left needle.
3 Bring yarn under right needle and through stitch…

4 …to form a new stitch on left needle. Pull stitch off right needle.

BASICS

KNIT, PURL IN ROW BELOW (k1b, p1b)

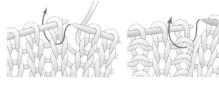

1 Instead of working into next stitch on left needle, work into stitch directly below it.

2 Pull stitch off left needle and let it drop.

KNIT THROUGH BACK LOOP (k1 tbl)

1 With right needle behind left needle and right leg of stitch, insert needle into stitch…

2 …and knit.

Right-side rows: k1 tbl, p1; Wrong-side rows: k1, p1 tbl.

PURL THROUGH BACK LOOP (p1 tbl)

1 With right needle behind left needle, insert right needle into stitch from left to right…

2 …and purl.

K1 tbl, p1 tbl rib

BASICS

GAUGE

10cm/4"

24 *GET GAUGE!*

18

• *over stockinette stitch*
• *after blocking*

• Cast on a minimum of 5" worth of stitches.
• Work 2 rows of **knit**, continue to work in pattern specified for 5", then work 2 rows of knit.

Measure the swatch
• Steam or wash the swatch as you will the garment; after drying, measure the swatch, then count the stitches and the rows in 4".
• If your stitches number less than the pattern's, your stitches are too large and you should try a swatch with a smaller-sized needle.
• If your stitches number more than the pattern's, your stitches are too small and you should try a swatch with a larger-sized needle.

• If your rows number 1 or 2 less than the pattern's, try a swatch with the next smaller-sized needle. This may give you the correct row gauge without affecting the stitch gauge.
• If your rows number 1 or 2 more than the pattern's, try a swatch with the next larger-sized needle. This may give you the correct row gauge without affecting the stitch gauge.

TIP
Even if your gauge swatch is correct, don't stop measuring. Periodically measure the piece you are working on. Your gauge can change as you are working.

BLOCKING

All swatches and knit pieces should be blocked. This sets the stitches and improves the hand of the knit fabric. Steam, mist with water, or wash, then lay the piece flat to dry. Lace is usually pinned out when damp; other knits can be patted into shape.

CARE

Most yarn labels offer care instructions. The most common care symbols are defined here. Hand-washing is often your best option; it takes only a few minutes. After each washing, block your knit by laying it flat to dry. **Never** hang a sweater, it should be folded and placed on a shelf or in a drawer.

Wool Cycle 40 Degrees
Do Not Wring

Do Not Wash

Hand Wash

Dry Clean

Do Not
Dry Clean

Do Not
Tumble Dry

Tumble Dry

BASICS

JOINING NEW YARNS

1 Work until approximately an 8" tail of yarn is left.

2 Leaving a 6" tail, hold new yarn beside previous yarn tail…

3 …and knit 3 stitches using both yarns. Drop short tail and continue with new yarn (as shown). After a few rows, darn in ends along purl bumps.

SPLICING

Splicing eliminates the need to darn in ends when joining in a new skein of wool. Separate the plies of the last 3–4" of both the old end and the new skein. Break off (do not cut) half of the plies on each end.

Overlap two ends in one palm. Spit into your other palm and rub your hands together briskly until you can feel heat—about 15 seconds. This join will hold after it is knit into fabric; until then, avoid pulling on it.

DARNING IN ENDS

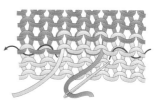

Darning in ends
With a blunt needle, weave each yarn through purl bumps for 5–6 stitches: new yarn toward beginning of row, old yarn toward end of row.

BASICS

USING MARKERS

Markers make it easy
• **to count stitches:** When casting on many stitches, place a marker every 20 stitches (or so).
• **to catch mistakes while they are small:** Place a marker between pattern repeats: if you don't have the correct number of stitches to complete the repeat, check for a mistake before going on.

• **to remember:** Place a marker between stitch panels, between a border and the main pattern, or at an increase/decrease.
• **to count rows:** Place a separating marker, a safety pin, or a piece of cotton thread into a stitch.

When you come to a marker on the needle, remember why it is there, then slip it from left needle to right needle.

USING STITCH HOLDERS

• When instructed to "place (or leave) stitches on hold," slip the stitches (purlwise) to a stitch holder, a spare knitting needle, or a piece of yarn; do **not** bind off. Until these stitches are slipped back onto a needle and

bound off, they are referred to as *live stitches.*
• When stitches are slipped from the holder back onto the needle, orient the stitches correctly.

Ring markers, separating markers, coilless safety pins, and thread markers

WINDING YARN

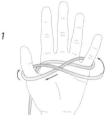

1

2

Butterfly wrap

Center-pull ball

Butterfly

Wrap yarn in figure-8 fashion around fingers 6–8 times (1). Remove wrap from hand. Hold one wing of butterfly between thumb and 2 fingers of left hand; other end of wing stays free. Begin winding yarn around thumb, wing, and fingers. After 10–12 wraps, slip fingers out, but keep thumb in place, turn ball slightly, replace fingers, and wind again. Repeat this process, gradually building a round ball of yarn (2). When finished, tuck end under last set of wraps, and free thumb and fingers. To start knitting, pull butterfly, and yarn will feed from center of ball.

Make small butterflies when using short lengths (less than 5 yards) of yarn for colorwork.

BASICS

UNDERSTANDING PATTERN SPECIFICATIONS

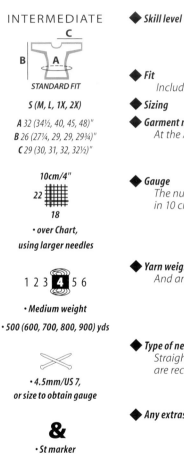

INTERMEDIATE

STANDARD FIT

S (M, L, 1X, 2X)

A 32 (34½, 40, 45, 48)"
B 26 (27¼, 29, 29, 29¾)"
C 29 (30, 31, 32, 32½)"

10cm/4"

22

18

• over Chart,
using larger needles

1 2 3 **4** 5 6

• **Medium weight**

• **500 (600, 700, 800, 900) yds**

• **4.5mm/US 7,**
or size to obtain gauge

&

• **St marker**

◆ *Skill level*

◆ *Fit*
    Includes ease (additional width) built into pattern.

◆ *Sizing*

◆ *Garment measurements*
    At the A, B, and C lines on the fit icon.

◆ *Gauge*
    The number of stitches and rows you need
    in 10 cm or 4", worked as specified.

◆ *Yarn weight*
    And amount in yards.

◆ *Type of needles*
    Straight, unless circular or double-pointed
    are recommended.

◆ *Any extras*

BASICS

MEASURING

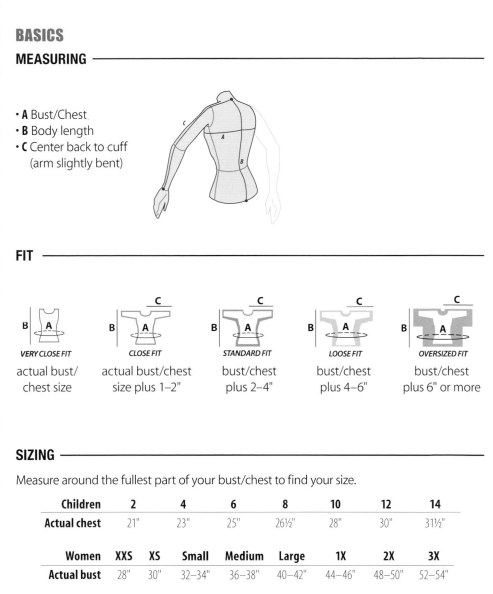

- **A** Bust/Chest
- **B** Body length
- **C** Center back to cuff
  (arm slightly bent)

FIT

VERY CLOSE FIT	CLOSE FIT	STANDARD FIT	LOOSE FIT	OVERSIZED FIT
actual bust/ chest size	actual bust/chest size plus 1–2"	bust/chest plus 2–4"	bust/chest plus 4–6"	bust/chest plus 6" or more

SIZING

Measure around the fullest part of your bust/chest to find your size.

Children	2	4	6	8	10	12	14
Actual chest	21"	23"	25"	26½"	28"	30"	31½"

Women	XXS	XS	Small	Medium	Large	1X	2X	3X
Actual bust	28"	30"	32–34"	36–38"	40–42"	44–46"	48–50"	52–54"

Men	Small	Medium	Large	1X	2X
Actual chest	34–36"	38–40"	42–44"	46–48"	50–52"

15

BASICS

UNDERSTANDING YARN WEIGHT CATEGORIES

Yarn Weight

1	**2**	**3**	**4**	**5**	**6**
Super Fine	*Fine*	*Light*	*Medium*	*Bulky*	*Super Bulky*

Also called

Sock	Sport	DK	Worsted	Chunky	Bulky
Fingering	Baby	Light-	Afghan	Craft	Roving
Baby		Worsted	Aran	Rug	

Stockinette Stitch Gauge Range 10cm/4 inches

27 sts	23 sts	21 sts	16 sts	12 sts	6 sts
to	to	to	to	to	to
32 sts	26 sts	24 sts	20 sts	15 sts	11 sts

Recommended needle (metric)

2.25 mm	3.25 mm	3.75 mm	4.5 mm	5.5 mm	8 mm
to	to	to	to	to	and
3.25 mm	3.75 mm	4.5 mm	5.5 mm	8 mm	larger

Recommended needle (US)

1 to 3	3 to 5	5 to 7	7 to 9	9 to 11	11 and
					larger

Locate the Yarn Weight and Stockinette Stitch Gauge Range over 10cm to 4" on the chart. Compare that range with the information on the yarn label to find an appropriate yarn. These are guidelines only for commonly used gauges and needle sizes in specific yarn categories.

GAUGE

10 cm
10 cm — 25 rows
19 sts

7 UK — 4½ mm
7 US

NEEDLES

MEDIUM
4
MOYEN
MEDIO

COMPANY
YARN NAME

100% Merino Wool
100% Merino Wolle
100% Merino Laine

50g

Approx Length 87m (95 yds)

SHADE	LOT
540	**200**

5 013712 834028

Warm (40° C) Wool Cycle, minimum machine action.

Cool iron

Do not bleach

Dry cleanable in certain solvents Consult cleaner

Do not tumble dry Dry flat out of direct heat and sunlight

A yarn label can tell you a lot.

BASICS

NEEDLE & HOOK SIZES

US	MM	HOOK
0	2	A
1	2.25	B
2	2.75	C
3	3.25	D
4	3.5	E
5	3.75	F
6	4	G
7	4.5	7
8	5	H
9	5.5	I
10	6	J
10½	6.5	K
11	8	L
13	9	M
15	10	N
17	12.75	

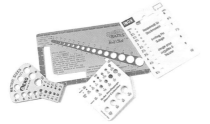

WEIGHT & MEASUREMENT CONVERSIONS

¾ oz		20 g
1 oz		28 g
1½ oz	**=**	40 g
1¾ oz	**=**	50 g
2 oz		60 g
3½ oz		100 g

		X		=	
centimeters			0.394		inches
grams			0.035		ounces
inches			2.54		centimeters
ounces			28.6		grams
meters			1.1		yards
yards			.91		meters

Bind-offs

BIND-OFFS

BIND OFF KNITWISE

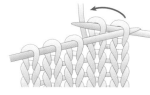

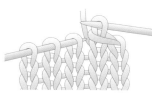

1 Knit 2 stitches as usual.
2 With left needle, pass first stitch on right needle over second stitch…

… and off needle: 1 stitch bound off (see above).
3 Knit 1 more stitch.
4 Pass first stitch over second. Repeat Steps 3–4.

TIPS
• *Since 2 stitches must be on the right needle before you can bind off 1 stitch, to bind off 10 stitches, you must work 11 stitches. Only count stitches as bound off when they have been pulled off the right needle.*

• *Usually the bind-off should be as elastic as the rest of the knitting. To avoid binding off too tightly, bind off with a larger needle or use Suspended Bind-off.*

BIND OFF PURLWISE

Work Steps 1–4 of *Bind off Knitwise* EXCEPT, *purl* the stitches instead of knitting them.

SUSPENDED BIND-OFF

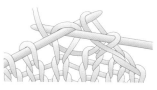

This method makes it very difficult to bind off too tightly.
1 Work (knit or purl) 2 stitches.
2 With left needle, pass first stitch on right needle over second stitch, but leave on left needle.

3 Work next stitch (shown above).
4 Slip both stitches from left needle.
5 Work next stitch.
Repeat Steps 2–5, ending with Step 4.

BIND OFF IN PATTERN

k2, p2 rib bound off in pattern   *k2, p2 rib bound off knitwise*

As you work the bind-off row for fabrics other than stockinette and garter stitch, knit or purl the stitches as the pattern requires. The bind-off (above left) is more attractive and flexible than in all-knit (above right).

FASTEN OFF

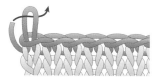

Work bind-off until only 1 stitch remains on right needle. If this is the last stitch of a row, cut yarn and fasten off stitch as shown above. Otherwise, this is the first stitch of the next section of knitting.

BIND-OFFS

3-NEEDLE BIND-OFF

Bind-off ridge on wrong side
1 With stitches on 2 needles, place **right sides together**.
* Knit 2 stitches together (1 from front needle and 1 from back needle); repeat from * once more (as shown).
2 With left needle, pass first stitch on right needle over second stitch and off right needle.

3 Knit next 2 stitches together.
4 Repeat Step 2.
5 Repeat Steps 3 and 4, end by drawing yarn through last stitch.

3-needle bind-off with ridge on wrong side

Bind-off ridge on right side
Work as for ridge on wrong side, EXCEPT, with **wrong sides together**.

3-needle bind-off with ridge on right side—a decorative treatment

BIND OFF WITH CROCHET HOOK

1 Insert hook into first stitch as if to knit, catch yarn and bring through stitch, pull stitch off knitting needle—one loop on hook.

2 Insert hook into next stitch as if to knit, catch yarn and bring through stitch and loop on hook, pull stitch off knitting needle—one loop on hook.

3 Repeat Step 2, end by drawing yarn through last stitch.

BIND-OFFS

EZ'S SEWN BIND-OFF

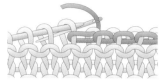 

Leave a long end of yarn and thread it in a blunt sewing needle. *1* Insert blunt needle into next 2 stitches **as if to purl** and pull through, leaving stitches on knitting needle.

2 Insert blunt needle into first stitch **as if to knit** and pull stitch off knitting needle. Repeat Steps 1–2.

TIPS
For the length of the sewing yarn, allow 3 times the width of the edge to be bound off.
EZ is Elizabeth Zimmermann who recommended this bind-off for garter stitch in **Knitting Without Tears.**

EZ's sewn bind-off on garter stitch

TUBULAR BIND-OFF FOR K1, P1 RIB (OR DOUBLE KNITS)

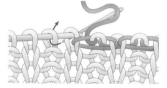  

Leave a long end of yarn and thread it in a blunt sewing needle. Assuming the first stitch is a knit stitch, bring yarn through it **as if to purl**, leave stitch on knitting needle. *1* Take blunt needle **behind knit stitch**, between first 2 stitches, and

through purl stitch **as if to knit**. Leave stitches on knitting needle. *2* Bring yarn around to front and through knit stitch **as if to knit**; pull stitch off knitting needle.

3 Take blunt needle in front of purl stitch and through knit stitch **as if to purl**. Leave stitches on knitting needle.

  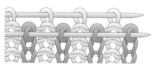

4 Bring yarn through purl stitch **as if to purl**; pull stitch off knitting needle. *5* Repeat Steps 1–4. Adjust tension.

Tubular bind-off on k1, p1 rib.

Alternative method
Divide the stitches onto 2 double-pointed needles: the knits on the front needle, the purls on the back needle.

Buttons, Buttonholes & Zippers

BUTTONS, BUTTONHOLES & ZIPPERS

1-ROW BUTTONHOLE

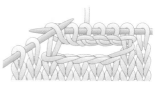

1 (Right-side row) Bring yarn to front and *slip 1 purlwise.* Take yarn to back and leave it there. * Slip next stitch, then pass previously slipped stitch over it; repeat from * for each buttonhole stitch. Put last slipped stitch back onto left needle.

2 Turn work. Bring the yarn to back and *cable cast on* as follows: * Insert right needle between first and second stitches on left needle, wrap yarn as if to knit, pull loop through and place it on left needle; repeat from * until you

have cast on 1 stitch more than was bound off.
3 Turn work. Bring yarn to back, slip first stitch from left needle, pass extra cast-on stitch over it, and tighten.

NOTE
 In Step 2, try leaving yarn in front and cable cast-on as if to purl. The result is shown in the photo below.

2-ROW BUTTONHOLE

Row 1 (Right-side) Work 2 stitches. With left needle, pull right stitch over the left and off needle (1 stitch bound off). * Work 1, pull first stitch over work-1; repeat from * for each bound-off buttonhole stitch.

Row 2 Cast on same number of stitches that were bound off, using *loop cast-on.*

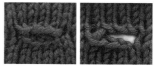

Top: 1-row and 2-row buttonholes Bottom: 3-row, 3-row alternate, and eyelet buttonholes.

3-ROW BUTTONHOLE

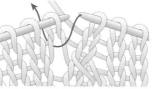

Row 1 (Right-side) *SSK, yarn over* twice (as shown).
Row 2 Purl into first yarn-over, drop second off needle.

Row 3 Knit into yarn-over space in row below. Pull stitch off left needle and let it drop.

EYELET BUTTONHOLE

Row 1 (Right-side) *SSK, yarn over* (as shown).
Row 2 Purl into yarn-over.

BUTTONS, BUTTONHOLES & ZIPPERS

ALTERNATE 3-ROW BUTTONHOLE

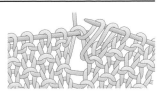

Illustrations show buttonhole worked in seed stitch.
Row 1 (Right-side) *Yarn over.*

Row 2 (Wrong-side) Work to yarn-over; with yarn in front, slip yarn-over to right needle, then yarn over again.

Row 3 Work to 1 stitch before yarn-overs, slip 1 knitwise, knit yarn-overs together but leave on left needle (as shown), pass slipped stitch over stitch just made, then knit yarn-overs together with next stitch on left needle.

BUTTONHOLE PLACEMENT

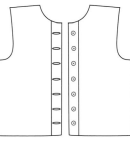

In *Jean Frost Jackets*, the left front or left buttonband is worked first, allowing you to work out button placement before you make any buttonholes.

TIP
For a woman's garment, adjust button placement so one button aligns with high point of the bust.

Often you are given specific instructions for placing the top and bottom buttons. To place the remaining buttons evenly between these two, measure the distance and divide by the number of remaining buttons plus 1. If 5 buttons remain, divide the distance (say 15") by 5 + 1; 15 divided by 6 equals 2.5: center a button every 2½".

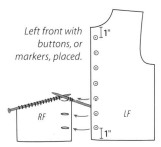

Left front with buttons, or markers, placed.

RF   LF

Right front follows: work buttonholes to match button placement.

BUTTON LOOP

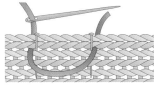
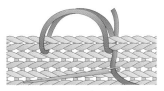

Mark position for top and bottom of loop.
1 Bring yarn needle up at one marker and down at the other, creating a loop.

2 Bring yarn up at first marker once more.

3 Work buttonhole stitch around both loops as follows: bring yarn to left of needle, then bring needle under loops and over yarn. Pull through and tighten.

BUTTONS, BUTTONHOLES & ZIPPERS

THREAD SHANK ——— 'CUFF-LINK' BUTTON ————————

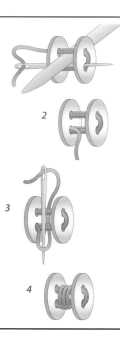

1

2

3

4

When sewing on flat buttons, accommodate the thickness of the sweater fabric by making a thread shank. Place a spacer (matchstick, darning needle, or toothpick) across the button and sew over it as you attach the button. Then remove the spacer, bring the needle between the button and fabric, and wrap the yarn around the shank several times before securing with a stitch or two.

Give your sweater a dual personality or protect fancy buttons from washing with 'cuff-link' buttons. Sew two buttons back to back using their own shanks or thread shanks (Steps 1–4). You must make buttonholes on both bands, but the versatility is worth the effort.

ATTACHING BUTTONS ——————————————————————

• Use a matching thread or yarn to attach buttons (remove a ply from the garment yarn, double it, and sew).
• No button should be wider than the button band.
• For added interest, sew 4-hole buttons onto a sweater using contrasting thread and…
   a plus sign
   an equal sign
   arrows (going every direction)
   boxes
   fill in all directions
…or maybe 2 triangles in a box
a bow tie or hourglass
the letters C, L, N, U, X or Z
or even the number 7.

BUTTONS, BUTTONHOLES & ZIPPERS

ZIPPERS

Sewing a zipper into a knit requires care. Although the knitted fabric has stretch, the zipper does not, and the two must be joined as neatly as possible to prevent ripples.

Here are the steps to follow for a smooth zipper placement:

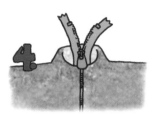

1 Measure the length of the opening. Select a zipper that matches the length of the opening or is a bit longer.
2 Pre-shrink your zipper by washing it as you will wash the garment.

3 Lay the garment flat, making sure that the sides match up.

4 If you are using a zipper that is too long, align at bottom, allowing extra to extend beyond neck.

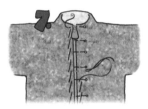

5 Pin the zipper in place. Be generous with the pins; extra care taken here makes the next steps easier.

6 Fold under any extra fabric at the top of the zipper and secure with pins.

7 Baste the zipper in place. When you are satisfied with the placement, remove the pins.

8 Sew in the zipper, making neat, even stitches.

9 If the zipper extends beyond the opening, trim extra length.

10 Reinforce stress points at the top and bottom edges.

Cables

CABLES

1/1 RIGHT TWIST (1/1 RT)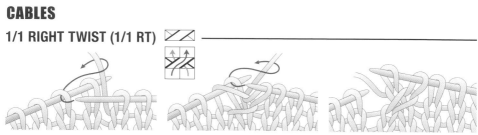

1 Bring right needle *in front of* first stitch on left needle. Knit second stitch but *do not remove* it from left needle.

2 Knit first stitch.

3 Pull both stitches off left needle. Completed 1/1 RT: 1 stitch crosses over 1 stitch and to the right. When worked with a cable needle, this is called a 1/1 Right Cross (1/1 RC).

1/1 LEFT TWIST (1/1 LT)

1 Bring right needle *behind* first stitch on left needle, and *to front between* first and second stitches. Knit second stitch, but *do not remove* it from left needle.

2 Bring right needle to right and in front of first stitch and knit first stitch.

3 Pull both stitches off left needle. Completed 1/1 LT: 1 stitch crosses over 1 stitch and to the left. When worked with a cable needle, this is called a 1/1 Left Cross (1/1 LC).

2/2 RIGHT CROSS (2/2 RC)

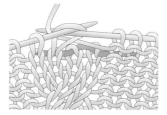

1 Slip 2 stitches onto a cable needle and hold (let it hang) to *back* of the knitting. Knit the next 2 stitches from the left needle.

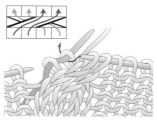

2 Then, holding the cable needle in your left hand, knit the 2 stitches from the cable needle.

2/2 RC: 2 stitches cross over 2 stitches and to the right

CABLES

2/2 LEFT CROSS (2/2 LC)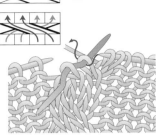

1 Slip 2 stitches onto a cable needle and hold (let it hang) to **front** of the knitting. Knit the next 2 stitches from the left needle.

2 Then, holding the cable needle in your left hand, knit the 2 stitches from the cable needle.

2/2 LC: 2 stitches cross over 2 stitches and to the left

a Purl to cable stitches

b Slip 2 stitches on cable needle and hold to front

c Knit 2 stitches from left needle

d Knit 2 stitches from cable needle

e Continue across

TIPS
• *All cable patterns use two basic techniques: the right cross (RC; also called the back cross or BC) and the left cross (LC; also called the front cross or FC). The only difference in working them is where you place the cable needle.*
• *2/2 means 2 stitches cross over 2 stitches. In a 2/4 RC, 2 stitches cross over 4; in a 4/2 RC, 4 stitches cross over 2.*

CABLES

CABLES IN SETS

Braid

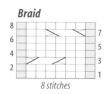

8 stitches

Horseshoe

10 stitches

Right and left crosses are often combined in cable patterns.

XOXO Cable

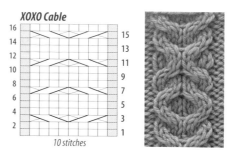

10 stitches

CABLES IN INTERVALS

The number of ribbed rows worked between crossings affects the look of the cable.

Varied Rows

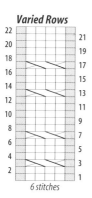

6 stitches

Repeat Rows 1–22

☐ K on RS, p on WS
☐ P on RS, k on WS

⬛ **2/2 RC**	Sl 2 to cn, hold to back, k2; k2 from cn
⬛ **2/2 LC**	Sl 2 to cn, hold to front, k2; k2 from cn
⬛ **2/4 RC**	Sl 4 to cn, hold to back, k2; k4 from cn
⬛ **2/4 LC**	Sl 2 to cn, hold to front, k4; k2 from cn
⬛ **4/2 RC**	Sl 2 to cn, hold to back, k4; k2 from cn
⬛ **4/2 LC**	Sl 4 to cn, hold to front, k2; k4 from cn

2/4, 4/2 UNEVEN CABLES

The 'halves' of a cross do not need to be an equal number of stitches.

2/4 Rope

Repeat Rows 19–24

Zig Zag

Repeat Rows 13–24

2/4, 4/2 Uneven

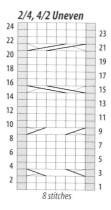

8 stitches

Twist & Turn

Repeat Rows 1–24

CABLES

CABLES & CHARTS

Cable patterns are just rearranged ribbings. In ribs you knit the knits and purl the purls. In a cable, every so many rows the ribs move to the right or to the left.

A cable needle (short and double-pointed) moves stitches off the knitting needle temporarily so that other stitches can be knit in their places. Charts show how many stitches to move and what to do with them.

The charts
Since the charts resemble the knitted fabric, after knitting a full repeat, train yourself to read the knitting as well as the chart.

Keeping track
Placing stitch markers between each pattern repeat is very helpful, at least until the patterns develop. Use a magnetic row finder (a flexible magnetic strip and accompanying metal sheet) or a large sticky note to mark the relevant row on the chart (covering the row above the one you are knitting).

One at a time
Before attempting a multi-cabled design, try swatching each of the charts separately. Cast on the number of stitches on the chart plus 2 or 3 garter stitches at each edge. Work 1 or 2 repeats of the pattern.

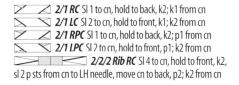

2/1 RC Sl 1 to cn, hold to back, k2; k1 from cn
2/1 LC Sl 2 to cn, hold to front, k1; k2 from cn
2/1 RPC Sl 1 to cn, hold to back, k2; p1 from cn
2/1 LPC Sl 2 to cn, hold to front, p1; k2 from cn
2/2/2 Rib RC Sl 4 to cn, hold to front, k2, sl 2 p sts from cn to LH needle, move cn to back, p2; k2 from cn

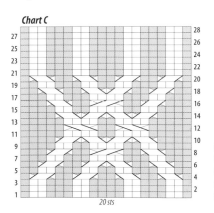

Chart C — 20 sts

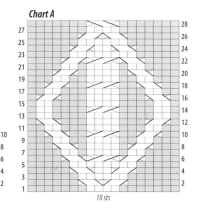

Chart B — 8 sts

Chart A — 18 sts

Cast-ons

CAST-ONS

LONG-TAIL CAST-ON, KNIT

Make a *slipknot* for the initial stitch, at a distance from the end of the yarn, allowing about 1½" for each stitch to be cast on.
1 Bring yarn between fingers of left hand and wrap around little finger as shown.

2 Bring left thumb and index finger between strands, arranging so tail is on thumb side, ball strand on finger side. Open thumb and finger so strands form a diamond.

3 Bring needle down, forming a loop around thumb.
4 Bring needle **under** front strand of **thumb loop**…

5 …up **over index finger yarn**, catching it…

6 …and bringing it **under** the front of **thumb loop**.

7 Slip thumb out of its loop, and use thumb to adjust tension on the new stitch. One knit stitch cast on.

CAST ON IN PATTERN

Repeat Steps 3–7 for each additional stitch.

K2, p2 rib cast on in k2, p2 pattern

K2, p2 rib cast on in knit

CAST-ONS

SLIPKNOT

1 Hold tail in left hand, working yarn in right.
2 Wrap working yarn around 2 or 3 fingers of left hand, forming a circle.
3 Insert needle in circle.

4 Draw working yarn through circle, forming a loop on needle (as shown).
5 Remove fingers and pull both tail and yarn to tighten loop.

6 Completed.

LONG-TAIL CAST-ON, PURL

1–3 Work as Steps 1–3 of *long-tail cast-on, knit.*
4 Bring needle **behind yarn** around index finger, **behind** front strand of **thumb loop**…

5 …up **over index finger yarn,** catching it…

6 …and bringing it **in front** of **thumb loop**…then backing it out **under thumb loop** and **index finger yarn**.

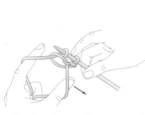 

7 Slip thumb out of its loop, and use thumb to adjust tension on the new stitch. One purl stitch cast on.

Repeat Steps 3–7 for each additional stitch.

TIPS
• *If you run out of cast-on tail before you are finished casting on, splice additional length and continue.*
• *If the cast-on tail is too long, cut off excess length.*
• *The long-tail cast-on has two sides: one looks smooth like outline stitch; the other side looks bumpy like purl stitches.*
• *The 'outline stitch' side is most commonly considered the right side.*

CAST-ONS

KNIT CAST-ON

1 Start with a *slipknot* on left needle (first cast-on stitch). Insert right needle into slipknot from front. Wrap yarn over right needle as if to knit.

2 Bring yarn through slipknot, forming a loop on right needle.
3 Insert left needle **under loop** and slip loop off right needle. One additional stitch cast on.

4 Insert right needle into the last stitch on left needle as if to knit. Knit a stitch and transfer it to the left needle as in Step 3. Repeat Step 4 for each additional stitch.

CABLE CAST-ON

Cable cast-on is useful when adding stitches within the work.

1–2 Work as for Steps 1 and 2 of *Knit Cast-on*.
3 Insert left needle in loop and slip loop off right needle. One additional stitch cast on.

4 Insert right needle **between** the last 2 stitches. From this position, knit a stitch and slip it to the left needle as in Step 3. Repeat Step 4 for each additional stitch.

LOOP CAST-ON (ALSO CALLED E-WRAP CAST-ON)

Left-slanting   *Right-slanting*

Often used to cast on a few stitches, as for a buttonhole
1 Hold needle and tail in left hand.
2 Bring right index finger under yarn, pointing toward you.

3 Turn index finger to point away from you.
4 Insert tip of needle under yarn on index finger (see above); remove finger and draw yarn snug, forming a stitch.
Repeat Steps 2–4 until all stitches are on needle.

Loops can be formed over index or thumb and can slant to the left or to the right. On the next row, work ***through back loop*** of right-slanting loops

CAST-ONS

CROCHET CAST-ON

1 Leaving a short tail, make a **slipknot** on crochet hook. Hold hook in right hand; in left hand, hold knitting needle on top of yarn and behind hook. With hook to left of yarn, bring yarn through loop on hook; yarn goes over top of needle, forming a stitch.

2 Bring yarn under point of needle and hook yarn through loop forming next stitch. Repeat Step 2 until 1 stitch remains to cast on. Slip loop from hook to needle for last stitch.

The crochet cast-on most resembles a bind-off.

INVISIBLE CAST-ON

A temporary cast-on
1 Knot working yarn to contrasting waste yarn. Hold needle and knot in right hand. Tension both strands in left hand; separate strands so waste yarn is over index finger, working yarn over thumb. Bring needle between strands and under thumb yarn so working yarn forms a yarn-over in front of waste yarn.

2 Holding both yarns taut, pivot hand toward you, bringing working yarn under and behind waste yarn. Bring needle behind and under working yarn so working yarn forms a yarn-over behind waste yarn.

3 Pivot hand away from you, bringing working yarn under and in front of waste yarn. Bring needle between strands and under working yarn, forming a yarn-over in front of waste yarn. Each yarn-over forms a stitch.
Repeat Steps 2–3 for required number of stitches. For an even number, twist working yarn around waste strand before knitting the first row.

PICKING UP STITCHES IN CHAIN

A temporary cast-on
1 With crochet hook and waste yarn, loosely chain the number of stitches needed, plus a few extra chains. Cut yarn.
2 With needle and main yarn, pick up and knit 1 stitch into the back 'purl bump' of the first chain.

Continue, knitting 1 stitch into each chain until you have the required number of stitches. Do not work into remaining chains.

REMOVING WASTE YARN

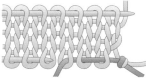

Later, untie knot, remove waste strand of invisible cast-on or unravel chain, and arrange bottom loops on needle.

CAST-ONS
TUBULAR CAST-ON

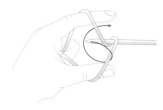

1 Leaving a tail approximately 4 times the width of the cast-on, fold the yarn over a needle 3–4 sizes smaller than main needle (1–2 sizes smaller than ribbing needle). Bring yarn between fingers of left hand and wrap around little finger as shown.

2 Bring left thumb and index finger between strands, arranging so tail is on thumb side. Open thumb and finger so strands form a diamond. Take needle **over index yarn, then under it.**

3 Bring needle **over thumb yarn** then **under it and under index yarn,** forming a purl stitch on needle.

4 Bring needle toward you, **over thumb yarn, under it,** and up between the two yarns.

5 Bring needle **over and under** the **index yarn.** Bring index yarn **under thumb yarn,** forming a knit stitch on the needle.

6 Take needle over index yarn, then under it. Repeat Steps 3–6.

7 End with Step 3. Note that knit stitches alternate with purl stitches.

8 Work 2 rows double knit as follows: *Row 1* * Knit 1 in back loop, slip 1 purlwise with yarn in front; repeat from *.
Row 2 * Knit 1, slip 1 purlwise with yarn in front; repeat from *.
9 Change to larger needles and work knit 1, purl 1 rib or repeat Row 2 for double-knit fabric.

Tubular cast-on for k1, p1 rib

Circular Knitting

CIRCULAR KNITTING

KNITTING IN ROUNDS

• After casting on, do not turn work. Knit into first cast-on stitch to join. Stop. Check to make sure that the cast-on does not spiral around the needle. If it does, undo the stitch, remove the spiral, then rejoin.
• Check your knitting at end of first and second rounds and make sure you have no twists.
• Mark the beginning of a round in one of three ways:
1 Place a marker on needle.
2 Use a safety pin in the fabric.
3 Weave your leftover cast-on tail between first and last stitch of round.

WORKING WITH 3 DOUBLE-POINTED NEEDLES (DPNS)

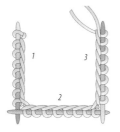
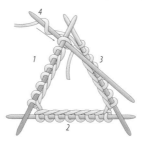

Cast stitches onto 1 dpn.
1 Rearrange stitches on 3 dpns. Check carefully that stitches are not twisted around a dpn or between dpns before beginning to work in rounds.

2 With a 4th dpn, work all stitches from first dpn. Use that empty dpn to work the stitches from the 2nd dpn. Use that empty dpn to work the stitches from the 3rd dpn—one round completed.

Place a marker between first and second stitch of first needle to mark beginning of round. Notice that you work with only 2 dpns at a time. As you work the first few rounds, be careful that the stitches do not twist between the needles.

WORKING WITH 4 DOUBLE-POINTED NEEDLES (DPNS)

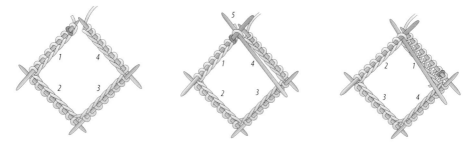

If instructions recommend working with a set of 5 dpns, arrange the stitches on 4 needles and knit with the fifth.

CIRCULAR KNITTING

CIRCLE CAST-ON

Use to cast on a few stitches at center of a flat circle.
1 Holding tail in right hand and yarn in left hand, make a circle.
2 Insert double-pointed needle in circle and draw yarn through, forming a **stitch** on needle. Do not remove fingers from loop.

3 Bring needle under and then over the yarn, forming a **yarn-over** on needle.

TIP
Swatches worked circularly from an 8-stitch circle cast-on with 8 yarn-over increases every other round: For a square, increase 2 stitches at 4 places; for an octagon, increase 1 stitch at 8 places.

4 Repeat Steps 2 and 3, ending with Step 2. To cast on an even number, yarn over before beginning the first round.
5 Arrange stitches on 3 or 4 double-pointed needles, pull tail slightly, then begin knitting around, working into the **back loops** of yarn-overs on the first round. Work several more rounds, then pull tail to close center.

CIRCLE BIND-OFF JOIN

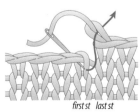

first st   last st

1 Fasten off last stitch in round.
2 Thread needle and join last stitch under first stitch of round for a neat edge.

CIRCULAR KNITTING
USING STEEKS

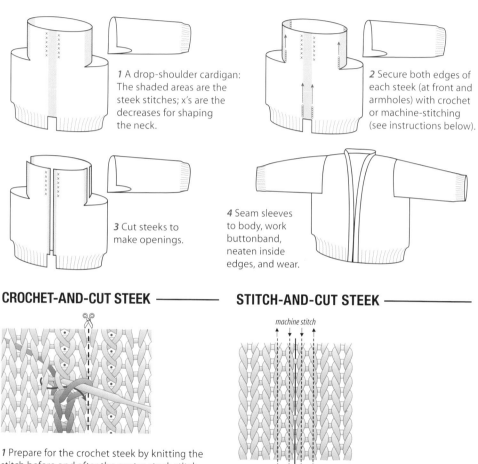

1 A drop-shoulder cardigan: The shaded areas are the steek stitches; x's are the decreases for shaping the neck.

2 Secure both edges of each steek (at front and armholes) with crochet or machine-stitching (see instructions below).

3 Cut steeks to make openings.

4 Seam sleeves to body, work buttonband, neaten inside edges, and wear.

CROCHET-AND-CUT STEEK

1 Prepare for the crochet steek by knitting the stitch before and after the center steek stitch *through the back loop*.
2 Holding yarn on the wrong side and crochet hook on the right side, crochet chain through each twisted stitch. Work a chain stitch in every round from bottom to top.
3 Cut through the center of the steek to form an opening.
Continue with Step 4, above.

STITCH-AND-CUT STEEK

machine stitch

cutting line

With contrasting yarn, mark center of steek by basting down center stitch. Make 2 parallel rows of stitching on each side of the basting yarn (stitch down the right or left leg of the stitches, not between the stitches). Cut through center stitch following basting yarn. Continue with Step 4, above.

Color

COLOR

STRANDED 2-COLOR KNITTING

*Two colors worked across a row form a color pattern: the unused color is carried (**stranded**) along the wrong side of the fabric. These 'carries' should not exceed 1 inch. **Weave** any carry longer than 1 inch along the wrong side.*

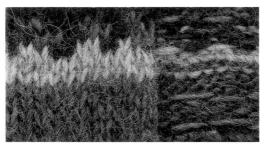

Right-side and wrong-side of stranded 2-color knitting.

TIPS
• *Stranded knitting can be worked back and forth (flat) or in the round.*
• *Carries should not be too tight or too loose so as not to affect the gauge or distort the fabric.*
• *Never twist colors between color changes in stranded knitting.*
• *Fair Isle is a style of stranded knitting.*

WEAVING THE CARRIES

The carried yarn is woven alternately above and below the working yarn on the purl side of the work. Weaving the carries results in a firmer fabric than stranding does.

From the knit side
To weave the carry above a knit stitch: Insert needle into stitch and under woven yarn, then knit the stitch as usual.

To weave the carry below a knit stitch: Insert needle into stitch and over woven yarn, then knit the stitch as usual.

From the purl side
To weave the carry above a purl stitch: Insert needle into stitch and under woven yarn, then purl the stitch as usual.

To weave the carry below a purl stitch: Insert needle into stitch and over woven yarn, then purl the stitch as usual.

COLOR

INTARSIA - PICTURE KNITTING

Color worked in areas of stockinette fabric: each area is made with its own length of yarn. Twists made at each color change connect these areas.

TIPS
• *Intarsia blocks are always worked back and forth, even in circular work.*
• *When bobbins are called for, make a **butterfly** or cut 3-yard lengths to prevent tangles.*
• *Work across a row and back before you untangle yarns.*

Right-side row   *Wrong-side row*

Making a twist:
Work across row to color change, pick up new color from under the old and work across to next color change.

COLOR CHARTS

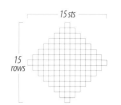

Square grid
Works if the knitted stitch gauge is close to the row gauge.

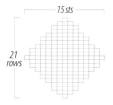

Knitter's grid
Works for the 5 stitch/7 row proportion of standard stockinette stitch.

Intarsia blocks

DUPLICATE STITCH

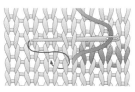

Duplicate stitch (also known as **swiss darning**) is just that: with a blunt tapestry needle threaded with a length of yarn of a contrasting color, cover a knitted stitch with an embroidered stitch.

TIP
Duplicate stitch is perfect for:
• *small color accents*
• *lines of color*
• *correcting mistakes*

TIPS
• *The shape of each grid should match the shape of the stitch so that the motif won't be distorted.*
• *Since stranded knitting is 'more square' than standard stockinette stitch, square grid can be used for most stranded knitting patterns.*

Crochet

CROCHET

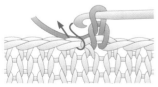

Top to bottom:
Slip stitch, Single, Half-double,
Double & Backward single

CHAIN STITCH (ch st, ch)

1 Make a slipknot to begin.
2 Catch yarn and draw through loop on hook.

First chain made. Repeat Step 2.

SLIP STITCH (sl st)

1 Insert the hook into a stitch, catch yarn, and pull up a loop.

2 Insert hook into the next stitch to the left, catch yarn and pull through both the stitch and the loop on the hook; 1 loop on the hook. Repeat Step 2.

SINGLE CROCHET (sc)

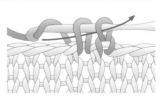

1 Insert hook into a stitch, catch yarn, and pull up a loop. Catch yarn and pull through the loop on the hook.
2 Insert hook into next stitch to the left.

3 Catch yarn and pull through the stitch; 2 loops on hook.

4 Catch yarn and pull through both loops on hook; 1 single crochet completed. Repeat Steps 2–4.

CROCHET

BACKWARD SINGLE CROCHET, CRAB STITCH

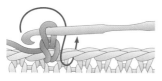  

1 Insert hook into a stitch, catch yarn, and pull up a loop. Catch yarn and pull a loop through the loop on the hook.
2 Insert hook into next stitch to right.

3 Catch yarn and pull through stitch only (as shown). As soon as hook clears the stitch, flip your wrist (and the hook). There are 2 loops on the hook, and the just-made loop is to the front of the hook (left of the old loop).

4 Catch yarn and pull through both loops on hook; 1 backward single crochet completed.

5 Continue working to the right, repeating Steps 2–4.

HALF DOUBLE CROCHET (hdc)

1 Insert hook into a stitch, catch yarn, and pull up a loop. Chain 2 (counts as first half double crochet).
2 Yarn over, insert hook into next stitch to the left (as shown). Catch

yarn and pull through stitch only; 3 loops on hook.
3 Catch yarn and pull through all 3 loops on hook: 1 half double crochet complete. Repeat Steps 2–3.

TIP
For more information on crochet—working in rows, working in rounds, increasing, and decreasing—see Edges & Borders, page 68.

DOUBLE CROCHET (dc)

1 Insert hook into a stitch, catch yarn, and pull up a loop. Chain 3 (counts as first double crochet).
2 Yarn over, insert hook into next stitch to the left (as shown). Catch yarn and pull through stitch only; 3 loops on hook.

3 Catch yarn and pull through 2 loops on hook.

4 Catch yarn and pull through remaining 2 loops on hook. Repeat Steps 2–4.

Decreases

DECREASES - single, right-slanting

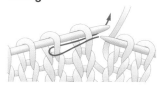

K2tog: before the same stitch on left, after the same stitch on right

K2tog

1 Insert right needle into first 2 stitches on left needle, beginning with second stitch from end of left needle.

2 Knit these 2 stitches together as if they were 1.
The result is a right-slanting decrease.

SSK: before the same stitch on left, after the same stitch on right

P2tog

1 Insert right needle into first 2 stitches on left needle.

2 Purl these 2 stitches together as if they were 1.
The result is a right-slanting decrease.

"SPACING DECREASES EVENLY"

Let's say there are **54 stitches** on the row and you are to **decrease 3:**
1 Since each decrease uses 2 stitches, multiply the number of decreases by 2: **3 x 2 = 6** stitches used to work the decreases. Subtract that number from the total number of stitches:
54 – 6 = 48 stitches to space between the decreases.
2 Divide that number by the number of decreases plus 1:
48 ÷ 4 = 12 stitches between **each** decrease.
3 To place the first and last decreases equidistant from the ends of the row, divide the number of stitches between increases by 2:
12 ÷ 2 = 6 stitches to work before the first and after the last increase.

NOTES

1 If the division in Step 2 or 3 does not result in a whole number, space the remaining stitches between the decreases as evenly as possible. For example, 44 ÷ 6 = 7 with 2 remaining. One way to space these stitches would be to knit one additional stitch after the first decrease and before the last.
2 The above formula pertains to single decreases, if you are doing a double decrease, each decrease uses 3 stitches.

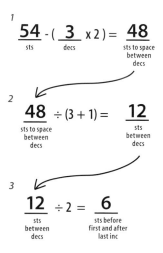

1

$$\frac{54}{\text{sts}} - (\ \frac{3}{\text{decs}}\ \text{x 2}\ ) = \frac{48}{\substack{\text{sts to space} \\ \text{between} \\ \text{decs}}}$$

2

$$\frac{48}{\substack{\text{sts to space} \\ \text{between} \\ \text{decs}}} \div (3 + 1) = \frac{12}{\substack{\text{sts} \\ \text{between} \\ \text{decs}}}$$

3

$$\frac{12}{\substack{\text{sts} \\ \text{between} \\ \text{decs}}} \div 2 = \frac{6}{\substack{\text{sts before} \\ \text{first and after} \\ \text{last inc}}}$$

DECREASES - single, left-slanting

SKP, sl 1-k1-psso

1 Slip 1 stitch knitwise from left needle onto right.
2 Knit 1 as usual.

3 Pass slipped stitch over knit stitch: 2 stitches become 1.

The result is a left-slanting decrease.

SSK

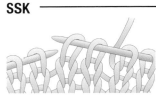  

1 Slip 2 stitches **separately** to right needle as if to knit.

2 Slip left needle into these 2 stitches from left to right and knit them together: 2 stitches become 1.

The result is a left-slanting decrease.

SSP

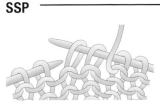 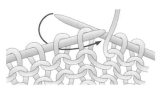 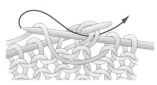

Use instead of p2tog-tbl to avoid twisting the stitches.

1 Slip 2 stitches **separately** to right needle as if to knit.

2 Slip these 2 stitches back onto left needle. Insert right needle through their 'back loops,' into the second stitch and then the first.

3 Purl them together: 2 stitches become 1.

The result is a left-slanting decrease.

DECREASES - double decreases

S2KP2, sl 2-k1-p2sso

1 Slip 2 stitches *together* to right needle as if to knit.

2 Knit next stitch.

3 Pass 2 slipped stitches over knit stitch and off right needle: 3 stitches become 1; the center stitch is on top.

S2KP2 decrease: a centered double decrease worked on the right side

The result is a centered double decrease.

SSPP2

1 Slip 2 stitches *separately* to right needle as if to knit.

2 Slip these 2 stitches back onto left needle. Insert right needle through their 'back loops,' into the second stitch and then the first, and slip the 2 stitches to right needle.

3 Purl next stitch.

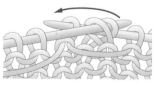

SSPP2 decrease: a centered double decrease worked on the wrong side

4 Pass 2 slipped stitches over purl stitch and off right needle: 3 stitches become 1; on the right side, the center stitch is on top.

DECREASES - double decreases

SK2P, sl 1-k2tog-psso

1 Slip 1 stitch knitwise.
2 Knit next 2 stitches together.
3 Pass the slipped stitch over the k2tog: 3 stitches become 1; the right stitch is on top.
The result is a left-slanting double decrease.

SK2P decrease: a left-slanting double decrease

K3TOG

1 Insert right needle into first 3 stitches on left needle, beginning with third stitch from tip.
2 Knit all 3 stitches together, as if they were 1.
The result is a right-slanting double decrease.

P3TOG

1 Insert right needle into first 3 stitches on left needle.
2 Purl all 3 stitches together, as if they were 1. The result is a right-slanting double decrease.

Right-slanting double decreases: k3tog (below), p3tog seen on the knit side (above)

SSSK

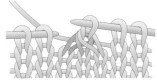

Work same as **SSK** EXCEPT:
1 Slip **3** stitches....
2 Slip left needle into these **3** stitches... **3** stitches become 1.
The result is a left-slanting double decrease.

SSSP

Work same as **SSP** EXCEPT:
1 Slip **3** stitches....
2 Slip these **3** stitches... into third stitch, then second, and then first.
3... **3** stitches become 1.
The result is a left-slanting double decrease.

Left-slanting double decreases: SSSK (below), SSSP seen on the knit side (above)

Edges & Borders

EDGES & BORDERS
NON-CURLING FABRICS

The edges of stockinette stitch roll—to the right side along a row of stitches, to the wrong side along a vertical column of stitches. For this reason, a non-curling stitch is usually worked for an inch or more at the beginning and end of a piece of stockinette stitch. If the side edges are not seamed, they too are often edged with a non-curling stitch.

K1, p1 rib
Multiple of 2 + 1
Right-side rows * K1, p1; repeat from *, end k1.
Wrong-side rows * P1, k1; repeat from *, end p1.
NOTE
On each row, you knit the knit stitches and purl the purl stitches.

K2, p2 rib
Multiple of 4 + 2
Right-side rows * K2, p2; repeat from *, end k2.
Wrong-side rows * P2, k2; repeat from *, end p2.

Garter stitch
Knit every row.

Seed stitch
Multiple of 2 + 1
All rows * K1, p1; repeat from *, end k1.
NOTE
On each row, you knit the purl stitches and purl the knit stitches.

EDGES & BORDERS

PICK UP AND KNIT VERTICALLY ────────── HORIZONTALLY ──────

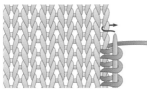

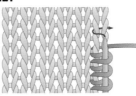

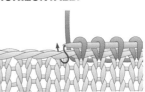

Insert needle 2 sizes smaller than garment needles *into* center of first stitch, catch yarn and knit a stitch.

For an even firmer edge, insert needle in space *between* first and 2nd stitches.

Along a horizontal edge, insert needle into center of every stitch.

PICK-UP RATES ────────────────────── PICK UP AND PURL ──────

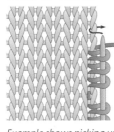

TIP
The ratio of picked-up stitches to rows is based on the pattern's row gauge. It is wise to test the formula by picking up stitches on your gauge swatch, working the border, and binding off.

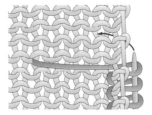

Example shows picking up 3 stitches for every 4 rows of stockinette stitch.

With wrong side facing and yarn in front, insert needle from back to front between first and second stitches, catch yarn, and purl.

Neckline or armhole

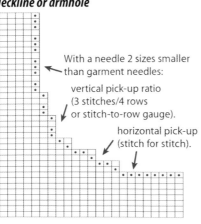

With a needle 2 sizes smaller than garment needles:

vertical pick-up ratio (3 stitches/4 rows or stitch-to-row gauge).

horizontal pick-up (stitch for stitch).

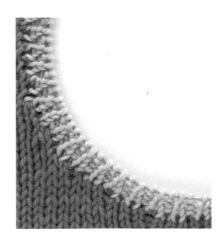

EDGES & BORDERS

CROCHET BORDERS

3 rows of single crochet worked back and forth

Crochet makes an excellent edge for knitting; it is firm and non-curling.

TIPS
• *The needle size chart on page 17 gives equivalent sizes for crochet hooks.*
• *For an edging, use a crochet hook equivalent to a needle that is 2 sizes smaller than the needle used to knit the piece.*
• *The rates at which you crochet into stitches will be the same as the pick-up rates explained on page 67.*

TIPS
• *Chain stitches are required at the beginning of the next row or round. This chain counts as the first stitch of the row or round.*
• *Because the height of the crochet stitches varies, chain 1 for single crochet, 2 for half double, and 3 for double crochet.*
• *When working crochet in rounds, join last stitch to first with a slip stitch, then make a chain of required length.*

CROCHET CORNERS

3-in-1 increase at corner

3-in-1 increase: Work 3 crochet stitches into 1 stitch. This rate of increase, repeated each row, works with all of the common crochet stitches.

2-to-1 decrease: Work a stitch to its last step, then work the next stitch to its last step, pull yarn through all loops on hook (shown above in single crochet).

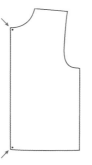

3 rounds of half double crochet with increases worked in 4 corners

Decrease at inside corner: 2-to-1 decrease work each side of V-point each row

EDGES & BORDERS

HEMS & CASINGS ———————————————————————————

Prepare for a hem by working a turning row.

Elongated row turn
Work a row with a needle 4–6 sizes larger than the garment needle.

Garter ridge turn
Purl a right-side row or knit a wrong-side row.

Picot turn
Right-side row * K2tog, yo; repeat from *, end k2tog.

Fold, baste hem, and your result is...

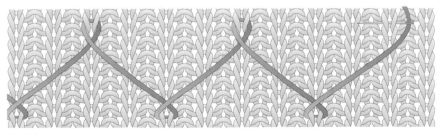

WAISTBAND CASING ———————————————————————————

Make casing for elastic waistband (as shown), place elastic in casing and sew ends together to fit waist. Block garment.

Extras

EXTRAS - surface stitch embellishments

BACKSTITCH

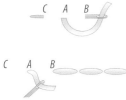

Bring needle out at A, down at B, and out again at C. Point C now becomes the point A of the next stitch.

BLANKET STITCH

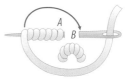

BULLION STITCH

Bring needle out at A, down at B, and back out at A, then wrap yarn around tip of needle several times. Keep yarn under tension as you pull needle through wraps. Take needle to back at B to complete stitch.

CHAIN STITCH

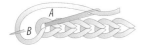

Chain stitch can be worked 2 ways:
1 Thread the yarn into a blunt needle, or …
2 … hold yarn on the wrong side of the fabric and a crochet hook on the right side.

COUCHING

1 Lay heavy yarn on the surface of the fabric.
2 Tack it down with little stitches in a finer yarn.

CROSS STITCH

A cross stitch is made in two steps: a diagonal stitch to the right crossed by a diagonal stitch to the left. Work each cross-stitch over 1 knit stitch.

DUPLICATE STITCH

Duplicate stitch (also known as **swiss darning**) is just that: with a blunt tapestry needle threaded with a length of yarn of a contrasting color, cover a knitted stitch with an embroidered stitch of the same shape.

FLY STITCH

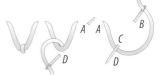

Bring needle out at A, form a loop, insert needle at B and bring out at C, determining the length of the stitch. Insert needle at D to fasten.

EXTRAS - surface stitch embellishments

FRENCH KNOT ———— LAZY DAISY ————————————

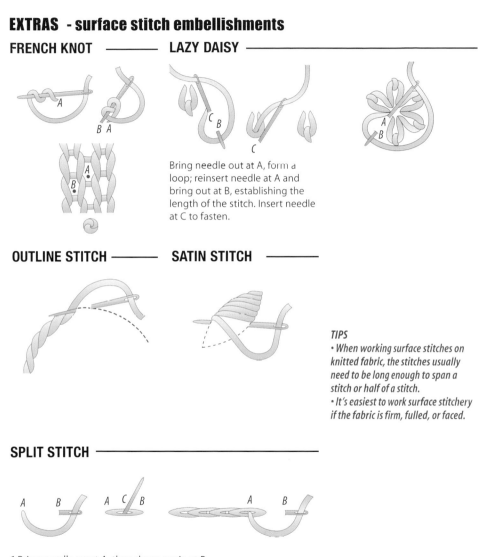

Bring needle out at A, form a loop; reinsert needle at A and bring out at B, establishing the length of the stitch. Insert needle at C to fasten.

OUTLINE STITCH ——— SATIN STITCH ————

TIPS
• When working surface stitches on knitted fabric, the stitches usually need to be long enough to span a stitch or half of a stitch.
• It's easiest to work surface stitchery if the fabric is firm, fulled, or faced.

SPLIT STITCH —————————————————————————————

1 Bring needle up at A, then down again at B.
2 Bring needle up at C, through center of stitch. Point C now becomes point A of the next stitch.

EXTRAS - beads & sequins
DRAWING-ON A BEAD OR SEQUIN

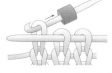

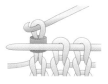

1 Knit the stitch you want to carry the bead. Insert a small crochet hook through the bead. (The bead's hole has to be big enough and the hook small enough.)

2 With the hook, pull the stitch off the needle and through the hole of the bead.

3 Replace the stitch on the needle, being careful not to twist it.

—SHAPING WITH BEADS

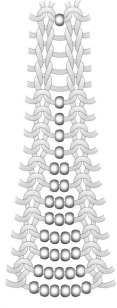

4 Tighten the yarn and continue.

Sequins and paillettes can be added in the same way.

KNITTING-IN BEADS OR SEQUINS

Using a loop of thread or fine wire, string required number of beads (or sequins) on yarn.

Slip bead up to back of work. As you knit the stitch, bring bead through to front of work.

Slide pre-strung beads between stitches.

EXTRAS - cords, tassels, fringe & more

TWISTED CORD

1 Cut strands 6 times the length of cord needed. Fold in half and knot cut ends together.
2 Place knotted end over a door knob or hook and right index finger in folded end, then twist cord tightly.

3 Fold cord in half, smoothing as it twists on itself. Pull knot through original fold to secure.

OVERHAND KNOT

TASSELS

1 Wrap yarn around a piece of cardboard that is the desired length of the tassel. Thread a strand of yarn under the wraps, and tie it at the top, leaving a long end.

2 Cut the wrapped yarn at lower edge. Wrap the long end of yarn around upper edge and thread the yarn through the top as shown. Trim strands.

I-CORD

Make a tiny tube of stockinette stitch with 2 double-pointed needles:
1 Cast on 3 or 4 sts.
2 Knit. Do not turn work. Slide stitches to opposite end of needle. Repeat Step 2 until cord is the desired length.

ATTACHING FRINGE

Cut lengths of yarn to twice desired length of fringe plus 1". Divide into groups of 2 or more strands.
1 Insert crochet hook from wrong side of work through a stitch at edge. Draw center of strands through, forming a loop.

2 Draw ends through loop. One fringe section complete.

75

EXTRAS - cords, tassels, fringe & more

POMPONS

1 Cut 2 pieces of cardboard half the desired width of the pompon.
2 Place a length of yarn between cardboard pieces.
3 Hold the pieces together and wrap yarn around them.

4 Tie the length of yarn tightly at one edge.
5 Cut the wrapped yarn on opposite side.

6 Remove cardboard, fluff, and trim pompon.
7 Use ties to attach.

WEAVING

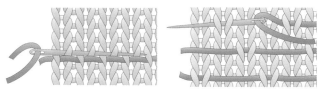

Weave lengths of accent yarn or ribbon through a knitted fabric for interesting effects. The knitted fabric can be worked a little or a lot looser than usual. Weave under and over each leg of every stitch (as shown above left), or at a larger scale (under 1 stitch and over 2 stitches as shown above right and in photo). The examples show stockinette stitch fabric, but other knit fabrics can expand the possibilities.

Cut lengths of weaving yarn to the approximate required length (including extra length for fringe on each end). The base fabric will draw up as weaving continues. Smooth it out as you work to maintain width of knit fabric.

This loosely-woven fabric shows ribbon at its silky best.

Grafts & Seams

GRAFTS & SEAMS

GRAFT IN STOCKINETTE

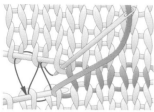

GRAFTING
An invisible method of joining live stitches. Useful at underarms, mitten tips, sock toes, and hats; also called Kitchener stitch.

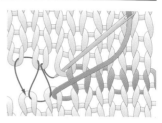

ON THE NEEDLES

1 Arrange stitches on 2 needles as shown.

2 Thread a blunt needle with matching yarn (approximately 1" per stitch).

3 Working from right to left, with right sides facing you, begin with Steps 3a and 3b:

3a Front needle: bring yarn through first stitch *as if to purl,* leave stitch *on needle.*

3b Back needle: bring yarn through first stitch *as if to knit,* leave stitch *on needle.*

4a Front needle: bring yarn through first stitch *as if to knit, slip off* needle; through next stitch *as if to purl,* leave stitch *on needle.*

4b Back needle: bring yarn through first stitch *as if to purl, slip off* needle; through next stitch *as if to knit,* leave stitch *on needle.*
Repeat Steps 4a and 4b until 1 stitch remains on each needle.

5a Front needle: bring yarn through stitch *as if to knit,* slip *off needle.*

5b Back needle: bring yarn through stitch *as if to purl,* slip *off needle.*

6 Adjust tension to match rest of knitting.

OTHER USES

Finished edges
Align stitches as shown. Graft over finished edges. Adjust tension.

Graft live stitches to rows
Compensate for different stitch and row gauges by occasionally picking up 2 bars (as shown above), instead of 1.

OFF THE NEEDLES

1 Place stitches on holding thread, remove needles, *block* pieces, and arrange as shown.

2 Thread a blunt needle with matching yarn (approximately 1" per stitch).

3 Working from right to left, with right sides facing you, begin with Steps 3a and 3b:

3a Lower piece: bring yarn from *back to front* through first stitch.

3b Upper piece: repeat Step 3a.

4a Lower piece: bring yarn from *front to back* through *previous stitch* worked, then from *back to front* through *next stitch.*

4b Upper piece: repeat Step 4a.
Repeat Steps 4a and 4b until 1 stitch remains on each piece.

5a Lower piece: bring yarn from *front to back* through stitch.

5b Upper piece: repeat Step 5a.

6 Remove holding thread and adjust tension to match rest of knitting.

The graft traces a row of stockinette.

GRAFTS & SEAMS

GRAFT IN GARTER

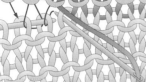 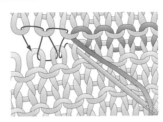

ON THE NEEDLES

1 Arrange stitches on 2 needles so stitches on lower, or front, needle come out of purl bumps and stitches on the upper, or back, needle come out of smooth knits.

2 Thread a blunt needle with matching yarn (approximately 1" per stitch).

3 Working from right to left, begin with Steps 3a and 3b:

3a Front needle: bring yarn through first stitch *as if to purl,* leave stitch *on needle.*

3b Back needle: repeat Step 3a.

4a Front needle: bring yarn through first stitch *as if to knit, slip off* needle; through next stitch *as if to purl, leave on* needle.

4b Back needle: repeat Step 4a. Repeat Steps 4a and 4b until 1 stitch remains on each needle.

5a Front needle: bring yarn through stitch *as if to knit,* slip *off needle.*

5b Back needle: repeat Step 5a.

6 Adjust tension to match rest of knitting.

TIP

When grafting a pattern stitch, practice by tracing the row in your swatch with duplicate stitch in a contrasting color. Then use that as your guide.

OFF THE NEEDLES

1 Place stitches on holding thread, remove needles, *block* pieces, and arrange so stitches on lower piece come out of purl bumps and stitches on the upper piece come out of smooth knits.

2 Thread a blunt needle with matching yarn (approximately 1" per stitch).

3 Working from right to left, begin with Steps 3a and 3b:

3a Lower piece: bring yarn from *back to front* through first stitch.

3b Upper piece: bring yarn from *front to back* through first stitch.

4a Lower piece: bring yarn from *front to back* through *previous stitch* worked, then from *back to front* through *next stitch.*

IN SEED STITCH

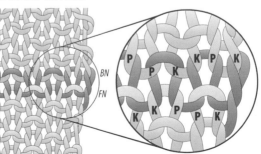

K knitwise   *BN* back-needle stitches
P purlwise   *FN* front-needle stitches

4b Upper piece: bring yarn from *back to front* through *previous stitch* worked, then from *front to back* through *next stitch*
Repeat Steps 4a and 4b until 1 stitch remains on each piece.

5a Lower piece: bring yarn from *front to back* through stitch.

5b Upper piece: bring yarn from *back to front* through stitch.

6 Remove holding thread and adjust tension to match rest of knitting.

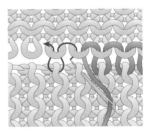

Graft live stitches to rows
In *garter stitch*, match a stitch and a ridge (2 rows).

GRAFTS & SEAMS

MATTRESS STITCH ───

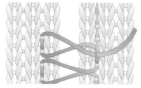

TIP
Block pieces before seaming.

Mattress stitch

Mattress stitch seams are good all-purpose seams. They require edge stitches (which are taken into the seam allowance).
1 Place pieces side by side, with right sides facing you.
2 Thread blunt needle with matching yarn.
3 Working between edge stitch and next stitch, pick up 2 bars.
4 Cross to opposite piece, and pick up 2 bars.
5 Return to first piece, work into the hole you came out of, and pick up 2 bars.
6 Return to opposite piece, go into the hole you came out of, and pick up 2 bars.
7 Repeat Steps 4 and 5 across, pulling thread taut as you go.

Garter ridge join

GARTER RIDGE JOIN ───

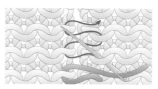

Join **garter stitch** edges this way for a nearly invisible seam.
1 Place pieces side by side, with right sides facing you.
2 Thread blunt needle with yarn to match garment.
3 Pick up or catch a lower garter ridge from one piece (right piece, above).
4 Cross to matching place on opposite piece and pick up or catch an upper garter ridge (left piece, above).
5 Repeat Steps 3 & 4. Pull thread taut, pulling pieces together as you go.

SEAMS IN RIBBING ───────────────

Any combination of knits and purls can be seamed in a way that makes the rib appear continuous. Most instructions will have you balance the rib: cast on 2 stitches + 1 for k1, p1 rib so right-side rows end with a k1, or cast on 4 stitches + 2 for k2, p2 rib so right-side rows end with a k2. In the first 2 examples below, seam one-half stitch in from the edge, and in the knit-to-purl seam, 1 stitch from the edge to create continuous k1, p1 rib.

Knit-to-knit seam

Purl-to-purl seam

Knit-to-purl seam

GRAFTS & SEAMS

SLIP-ST CROCHET SEAM   BACKSTITCH SEAM ——   OVERCAST SEAM ——

Place right sides together and **slip-stitch crochet** through both layers, working between the edge stitch and the next stitch.

Place right sides together and **backstitch,** allowing the finished seam some flexibility.

Overcast (whip stitch) seams are perfect for quick seams. And work well for very textured yarns.

TIPS
- *When seaming, use the garment yarn unless it is difficult to work with (too heavy, too textured, or too fragile). In that case, use a finer, smoother, or stronger yarn in a similar color and fiber.*
- *When seaming a piece, begin at hemline and work upward. Align edges and pin seams before you begin.*
- *Pinning is especially helpful when setting-in sleeves.*

Increases

INCREASES - worked between stitches
YARN-OVER (yo)

Between knit stitches
Bring yarn under needle to the front, take it over the needle to the back and knit the next stitch.

Completed yo increase. For a complete review of yarn-overs, see Basics, page 8.

Yarn-over worked before and after a stitch every other row: a decorative increase

LOOP CAST-ON

Left-slanting loop cast-on

Paired loop cast-on increases
Right-slanting loop on right side of stitch and left-slanting loop on left side of stitch.

Right-slanting loop cast-on
Work through the back loop on next row.

MAKE 1 LEFT (M1L), KNIT

Insert left needle from front to back under strand between last stitch knitted and first stitch on left needle. Knit, twisting strand by working into loop at back of needle.

Completed M1L knit: a left-slanting increase.

Make 1 left increase worked after same stitch every other row

INCREASES - worked between stitches

MAKE 1 RIGHT (M1R), KNIT

Insert left needle from back to front under strand between last stitch knitted and first stitch on left needle. Knit, twisting the strand by working into loop at front of the needle.

Completed M1R knit: a right-slanting increase.

M1R, knit worked before same stitch every other row

MAKE 1 LEFT (M1L), PURL

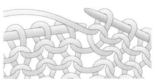

Insert left needle from front to back under strand between last stitch worked and first stitch on left needle. ***Purl***, twisting strand by working into loop at back of needle from left to right.

Completed M1L purl: a left-slanting increase.

M1L, purl worked before same stitch every other row

MAKE 1 RIGHT (M1R), PURL

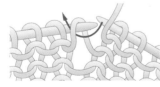

Work as for Make 1 Right, Knit, EXCEPT ***purl.***

Completed M1R purl: a right-slanting increase.

M1R, purl worked after same stitch every other row

87

INCREASES - worked into stitches

KNIT INTO FRONT AND BACK (kf&b)

1 Knit into the front of next stitch on left needle, but do not pull the stitch off the needle.
2 Take right needle to back, then knit through the back of the same stitch.

3 Pull stitch off left needle. Completed increase: 2 stitches from 1 stitch. This increase results in a purl bump after the knit stitch.

Kf&b worked after same stitch every other row

PURL INTO FRONT AND BACK (pf&b)

1 Purl into front of next stitch, but do not pull stitch off needle.
2 Take right needle to back, then through back of same stitch, from left to right...

3 ... and purl.

4 Pull stitch off left needle. Completed increase: 2 stitches from 1 stitch. This increase results in a purl bump before the stitch on the right side.

LIFTED INCREASE, KNIT OR PURL

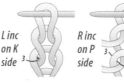

Work increase before stitch
Knit or purl into right loop of stitch in row below next stitch on left needle (1), then knit or purl into stitch on needle (2).

Work increase after stitch
Knit or purl next stitch on left needle, then knit or purl into left loop of stitch in row below this stitch (3).

Right (R) and left (L) increase combined: 3 stitches from 1 stitch, worked every other row

INCREASES - worked into stitches

KOK INCREASE (k1-yo-k1)

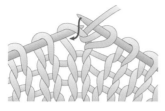

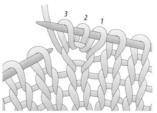

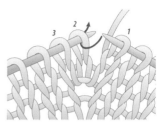

1 Knit 1, leaving stitch on left needle.
2 Bring yarn to front and over needle.
3 Knit into the stitch again.

Completed increase: 3 stitches from 1 stitch.

On next increase row, work KOK increase into center stitch of increase of previous increase row.

KOK increase worked every other row

"SPACING INCREASES EVENLY"

Let's say there are **48 stitches** on the row and you are to **increase 3.**

INCREASES WORKED BETWEEN STITCHES
1 Divide the total number of stitches by the number of increases:
48 ÷ 3 = 16 stitches between each increase.
2 To place the first and last increases equidistant from the ends of the row, divide the number of stitches between increases by 2: **16 ÷ 2 = 8** stitches to work before the first and after the last increase.

INCREASES WORKED INTO STITCHES
Since each increase is worked into a stitch, prepare for Step 1 by subtracting the number of increases from the total number of stitches: **48 - 3 = 45** stitches between the increases. Work Steps 1 and 2.

NOTE
In either case, if the division in Steps 1 or 2 does not result in a whole number, space the remaining stitches between the increases as evenly as possible. For example, 43 ÷ 5 = 8 with 3 stitches remaining. One way to space these stitches would be to knit one additional stitch before first, third, and fifth increase.

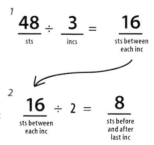

1
$$\underset{\text{sts}}{48} \div \underset{\text{incs}}{3} = \underset{\substack{\text{sts between} \\ \text{each inc}}}{16}$$

2
$$\underset{\substack{\text{sts between} \\ \text{each inc}}}{16} \div 2 = \underset{\substack{\text{sts before} \\ \text{and after} \\ \text{last inc}}}{8}$$

Lace

LACE & CHARTS

In most lace patterns, the number of stitches remains constant on each row. In these cases, when a yarn-over adds a stitch, a decrease removes another stitch. This yarn-over and decrease combination is called a ***pair***. A single yarn-over can be paired with a single decrease; 2 single yarn-overs can be paired with a double decrease.

The decreases used in lace patterns are familiar. The variety of patterns comes from the placement of yarn-overs and decreases. Most often both parts of the pair are on the same row and side by side, but they also can be separated by other stitches. In some patterns, yarn-overs are on one row, decreases on another.

Reading charts

Charts are invaluable when following the yarn-over/decrease relationships that are so crucial to the success and pleasure of lace knitting. If you're a beginning lace knitter or have had problems with lace, give these charted patterns a try.

Each square of the chart is one stitch (or one knitting operation, such as a k2tog or an SK2P). Each row of the chart shows a completed row of knitting.

The chart represents the right side of the fabric, so check the key to see how to work a certain symbol on the right side and on the wrong side. If a pattern has plain wrong-side rows (no increases or decreases), the lace chart may

show only the right-side rows and the key would tell how to work the wrong-side rows.

Read the chart in the same direction as you knit: the rows from bottom to top, right-side rows from right to left, wrong-side rows from left to right. (In circular knitting, all rows are right-side rows, therefore the chart is always read from right to left.)

Heavy lines set off a pattern repeat from any partial repeats or edge stitches. They function in the same way that asterisks do. In Chart 1 work the first stitch of the chart, then work the 12-stitch repeat until only 12 stitches remain, work the last 12 stitches of chart.

Chart 1

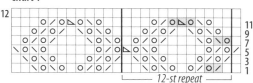

12-st repeat

It's simple to see the pairs here. The SK2P is a double decrease and pairs with 2 yarn-overs

Chart 2

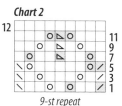

9-st repeat

Here the yarn-overs and decreases are on the same line but often separated by 1 or 2 knit stitches.

Chart 3

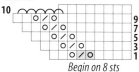

Begin on 8 sts

Each RS row has a yarn-over/ decrease pair plus an extra yarn-over resulting in an increase on the left edge. These 5 extra stitches are bound off on row 10.

☐ K on RS, p on WS	☑ K2tog
⊙ Yo	⌒ Bind off
◼ SK2P	◼ SSK

WS rows: Purl for Charts 1 and 2; knit for Chart 3, EXCEPT Row 10

TIPS

• *You can mark the neck or armhole shapings on your chart to see if the shaping breaks up any increase/decrease pairs. If so, eliminate both and simply knit or purl to the next pair.*
• *For a review of working yarn-overs, see Basics, page 8.*

LACE & CHARTS

Chart 1 Multiple of 12 sts + 1
Row 1 (RS) K1, * k1, [k2tog, yo] twice, k1, [yo, SSK] twice, k2; repeat from *.
Row 2 and all WS rows Purl.
Row 3 K1, * [k2tog, yo] twice, k3, [yo, SSK] twice, k1; repeat from *.
Row 5 K2tog, * yo, k2tog, yo, k5, yo, SSK, yo, SK2P; repeat from *, end last repeat SSK instead of SK2P.
Row 7 K1, * [yo, SSK] twice, k3, [k2tog, yo] twice, k1; repeat from *.
Row 9 K1, * k1, [yo, SSK] twice, k1, [k2tog, yo] twice, k2; repeat from *.
Row 11 K1, * k2, yo, SSK, yo, SK2P, yo, k2tog, yo, k3; repeat from *.
Repeat Rows 1–12.

Chart 2 Multiple of 9 sts
Row 1 (RS) * K2tog, k2, yo, k1, yo, k2, SSK; repeat from *.
Row 2 and all WS rows Purl.
Row 3 * K2tog, k1, yo, k3, yo, k1, SSK; repeat from *.
Row 5 * K2tog, yo, k5, yo, SSK; repeat from *.
Row 7 * K1, yo, k2, SK2P, k2, yo, k1; repeat from *.
Row 9 * K2, yo, k1, SK2P, k1, yo, k2; repeat from *.
Row 11 * K3, yo, SK2P, yo, k3; repeat from *.
Repeat Rows 1–12.

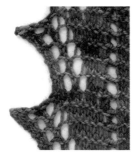

Chart 3 Begin on 8 stitches
Row 1 (RS) K4, yo, k2tog, yo, k2.
Rows 2, 4, 6, 8 (WS) Knit.
Row 3 K5, yo, k2tog, yo, k2.
Row 5 K6, yo, k2tog, yo, k2.
Row 7 K7, yo, k2tog, yo, k2.
Row 9 K8, yo, k2tog, yo, k2.
Row 10 Bind off 5 sts, k7—8 sts on needle.
Repeat Rows 1–10.

TIPS
• *If you run into a problem with the stitch count in a row, check for a missing yarn-over in the preceding row (see Basics, page 9).*
• *Practice working these patterns from the charts, referring to the written instructions only if you must. Soon charts will be your knitting language of choice.*
• *Charts make it easy to understand a pattern stitch before you knit it; to recognize, avoid, and correct errors; to enlarge or reduce a pattern stitch; to combine pattern stitches or their elements.*

Shaping

SHAPING - with short rows

REFINED SHORT ROWS

Each short row adds 2 rows of knitting across a section of the work. Since the work is turned before completing a row, stitches must be wrapped at the turn to prevent holes. Wrap and turn as follows:

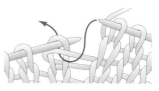

Knit side
1 With yarn in back, slip next stitch as if to purl. Bring yarn to front of work and slip stitch back to left needle (as shown). Turn work.
2 With yarn in front, slip next stitch as if to purl. Work to end.

3 When you come to the wrap on a following knit row, hide the wrap by knitting it together with the stitch it wraps.

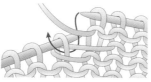

Purl side
1 With yarn in front, slip next stitch as if to purl. Bring yarn to back of work and slip stitch back to left needle (as shown). Turn work.
2 With yarn in back, slip next stitch as if to purl. Work to end.

3 When you come to the wrap on a following purl row, hide the wrap by purling it together with the stitch it wraps.

The first stitch of each short row is slipped (Step 2); this tapers the ends of short rows. When the wraps are hidden (Step 3), the mechanics of the shaping are almost invisible (see photo below).

SHORT-ROW SHOULDERS

Shape shoulders and neck with a series of short rows.

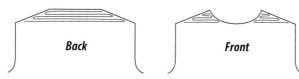

Back

Front

Create a smooth shoulder line with short rows. Usually short-row shoulders are not bound off and seamed, but are joined with 3-needle bind-off.

SHAPING - with short rows

STAIRSTEP SHOULDERS

Shape shoulders with a series of bind-offs.

Standard Stairstep

Refined Stairstep

Standard
A series of bind-offs are worked at the beginning of alternate rows.

Refined
To smooth steps: Work as for standard stairstep; but on non-bind-off rows, work a decrease on last 2 stitches, making sure its slant matches the shoulder's. (This decrease counts as first bound-off stitch.)

Stairstep bind-off is smoothed by a decrease worked on non-bind-off rows.

SHAPING SHORT-ROW SOCK HEELS

V-heel
Short rows begin at end of heel flap and lengthen to full width of heel.

Hourglass heel
Rows shorten from full width of heel then lengthen to full width of heel.

Hourglass heel in a baby sock

SHORT-ROW BUST DARTS

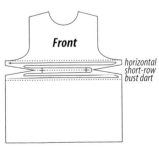

Front

horizontal
short-row
bust dart

This dart is worked much like the hourglass heel: rows shorten to the center of the dart, then lengthen to full width of garment.

Short-row bust darts are an easy way to improve fit for full figures.

97

SHAPING - with increases and decreases

DARTS

Waistline darts: balance decreases below the waistline with increases worked above it.

The shaping can be pairs of single right- and left-slanted decreases and increases…

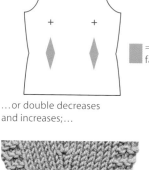

…or double decreases and increases;…

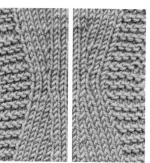

= no fabric

…or the shaping can be single right and left decreases and increases that mirror each other.

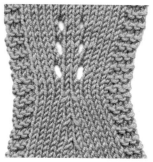

SSK and k2tog decrease pair; yo, k2, yo increase pair

S2KP2 decrease; KOK increase

K2tog decrease and M1L at right; SSK decrease and M1R at left

MITTENS

Add stitches from cuff to mid-palm to create a thumb gusset for a mitten or glove.

The flexibility of knitted fabric and the ease of shaping with increases, decreases, and short rows make knits the fabric of choice for comfort and fit.

SHAPING - with increases and decreases

NECKLINES

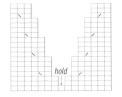

crew - round
Bind off center stitches then shape each side according to instructions, usually with a combination of bind-offs and decreases.

V-neck
Place center stitch on holder and decrease each side of center at a rate to achieve neck width in desired length.

REVERSE SHAPING

The shaping from one side of a garment is 'mirrored' on the opposite side.
When shaping you bind off at the beginning of a row. You bind off on right-side rows for a right edge, on wrong-side rows for a left edge. The slant of the decreases and increases should also be mirrored.

Reverse shaping is often found in necklines and armholes.

FULL-FASHIONED

Place decreases 1, 2, or more stitches in from the edge for a decorative line of decreases. The edge stitches are uninterrupted for a smooth pick up or seamline. Necklines, raglans and sleeve seams are common places to see this.

The slant of the decrease matches the slant of the edge

The slant of the decrease does not match the slant of the edge

Symbols & Charts

SYMBOLS

WORKING FROM CHARTS

Charts are graphs or grids of squares that represent the right side of knitted fabric. They illustrate every stitch and the relationship between the rows of stitches.

Squares contain knitting symbols.

The stitch key defines each symbol as an operation to make a stitch or stitches.

The pattern provides any special instructions for using the chart(s) or the key.

The numbers along the side of charts indicate the rows. A number on the right marks a right-side row, which is worked leftward from the number. A number on the left marks a wrong-side row that is worked rightward. Since many stitches are worked differently on wrong-side rows, the key will indicate that. If the pattern is worked circularly, all rows are right-side rows and worked from right to left.

Bold lines within the graph represent repeats. These set off a group of stitches that are repeated across a row. You begin at the edge of a row or where the pattern indicates for the required size, work across to the second repeat line, then repeat the stitches between the repeat lines as many times as directed, and finish the row.

The sizes of a garment are often labeled with beginning and ending marks on the chart. This avoids having to chart each size separately.

SYMBOL GLOSSARY

☐ *K on RS, p on WS*

☐ *P on RS, k on WS*

⊟ *P on RS, k on WS (on a color chart)*

⊙ *Yo*

⧹ *SSK on RS, SSP on WS*

⧸ *K2tog on RS, p2tog on WS*

⊻ *Right-slanting inc*   ⊼ *Left-slanting inc*

⊻ *Sl 1 with yarn at WS*

⊻ *Sl 1 with yarn at RS*

⊿ *K3tog on RS, p3tog on WS*

⊾ *SK2P*

▲ *S2KP2*

Ω *K1 tbl on RS, p1 tbl on WS*

B *Make bobble*

▇ *Sts do not exist in these areas of chart*

M *Make 1*

V *Inc 2*

⊛ *K1, wrapping yarn twice around needle*

⌒ *Bind off 1 st*

⧈ *1/1 LC, 1/1 LT*

⧈ *1/1 RC, 1/1 RT*

⧈ *1/1 LPC*

⧈ *1/1 RPC*

⧄⧄ ⧄⧄ *2/1 LC - RC*

⧄⧄ ⧄⧄ *2/1 LPC - RPC*

⧄ ⧄ *1/2 LC - 1/2 RC*

⧄ ⧄ *1/2 LPC - 1/2 RPC*

⧄ ⧄ *2/2 LC - RC*

⧄ ⧄ *2/2 LPC - RPC*

CHARTS

SAMPLE CHARTS

Basket weave pattern

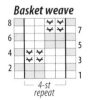

Basket weave

Stitch key
☐ K on RS, p on WS
▨ P on RS, k on WS
☑ Slip 1 purlwise with yarn at RS of work

└ 4-st ┘
repeat

Multiple of 4 sts + 2

Row 1 (RS) K1, *k2, p2; repeat from *, end k1.

Row 2 K1, *k2, p2; repeat from *, end k1.

Row 3 K1, *k2, slip 2 purlwise with yarn in front (sl 2 wyif); repeat from *, end k1.

Row 4 K1, *slip 2 purlwise with yarn in back (sl 2 wyib), p2; repeat from *, end k1.

Row 5 K1, *p2, k2; repeat from *, end k1.

Row 6 K1, *p2, k2; repeat from *, end k1.

Row 7 K1, *sl 2 wyif, k2; repeat from *, end k1.

Row 8 K1, *p2, sl 2 wyib; repeat from *, end k1.

Repeat Rows 1–8.

Twill pattern

Twill

Stitch key
☐ K on RS, p on WS
▨ K on WS
☑ Slip 1 purlwise with yarn at RS of work

└ 4-st ┘
repeat

Multiple of 4 sts + 2

Row 1 and all WS rows K1, p to last st, k1.

Row 2 (RS) K1, *k2, slip 2 with yarn in front (sl 2 wyif); repeat from *, end k1.

Row 4 K1, *k1, sl 2 wyif, k1; repeat from *, end k1.

Row 6 K1, *sl 2 wyif, k2; repeat from *, end k1.

Row 8 K1, *sl 1 wyif, k2, sl 1 wyif; repeat from *, end k1.

Repeat Rows 1–8.

INDEX

INDEX